TICK TOCK, LISTEN TO THE CLOCK TALK

by Sharlene Long-Booth

ABOUT THE AUTHOR

Born and raised in California, where I lived most of my life. Met and married my husband there as well. We moved to Las Vegas in 1996 and finished raising our daughters. After being a Real Estate Agent and an Escrow Officer for many years, I retired. We travel quite a bit and are just enjoying our life. I would make up stories and songs to entertain my granddaughters. Well, this one just resonated with me. Hence, my writing this storybook. Hope you will enjoy it as much as we do.

DEDICATION

To my wonderful and loving family for all their love and support, especially my amazing granddaughters, Nora, Hazel, and Sawyer, who are my inspirations.

ACKNOWLEDGMENTS

Thanks to everyone who patiently listened while I went on and on about this project.

Tick tock,
listen to the clock talk,

Get up you sleepy head,
Let's get out of bed.

Tick tock,
listen to the clock talk,

it's time to eat, wash your face.
and brush our teeth.

Tick tock,
listen to the clock talk,

It's such a sunny day. Let's go out and play.

Put on your
socks and shoes,
There is no time
to snooze.

Park
Nora Lane
Hazel way
Tick tock, listen to the clock talk,

Let's take a
walk, around
the block
or maybe
to the park.

Tick tock,
listen to the clock talk,

We'll run and play along the way,
until the end of day.

So many things
to do and see,
cars, trucks, fire hydrants,
and birds in trees.

Tick tock,
listen to the
clock talk,

Dinner we must eat,
vegetables and meat?
Anyone for a treat?

Tick tock,
listen to the clock talk,

The day is done,
We've had our fun.
Now we have been fed.
It's time for bed.

Tick tock,
listen to the clock talk,

So lay down your head.
A kiss good night, turn off the lights,
And listen to the clock talk.

"Good night."

"Good night, clock."